"This is a book written by a vibrant woman who is taking retirement seriously before it is too late. She is singing a song for all of us. In this journey of the mind, she brings the reader along with her no-nonsense language. Her guidance is sage, and the practical information and poems will bring many smiles of recognition. Reading this book is an illuminating step in the direction of happily confronting the aging years."

> – **Dr. Erving Polster**, founder and director of the Gestalt Training Center of San Diego and author of *Every Person's Life Is Worth a Novel*

"I have read Dr. Josefowitz's warm, humorous, self-disclosing book on retirement with great delight. While making you laugh, she makes you think about the important questions and issues concerning the challenges of retirement. Filled with Natasha's own experiences and insightful, inspiring poetry, this wonderful little book is for anyone facing the challenges and opportunities of retirement. It will make you smile and think."

> – **J. Adam Milgram, MA**, executive director of the Sam and Rose Stein Institute for Research on Aging, University of California at San Diego

"A wonderful, light-hearted look at the opportunities for adventure after retirement."

> – **B.J. Curry Spitler, PhD, LCSW**, founder of Age Concerns, an organization of care management and home care for the elderly

"A helpful, very comprehensive book for seniors who are approaching retirement. It will help them get a better grasp of some of the issues they might face, as well as prepare them for this next stage of life."

> – **David Myran**, staff psychiatrist at Baycrest Centre for Geriatric Care, Toronto

P9-DHN-074

ALSO BY NATASHA JOSEFOWITZ

*Too Wise to Want to Be Young Again: A Witty View of How to
Stop Counting the Years and Start Living Them*

RETIREMENT

Wise and Witty Advice
for Making It

The Next Great
Adventure

Natasha Josefowitz, PhD

Blue Mountain Press™
Boulder, Colorado

Copyright © 2005 by Natasha Josefowitz.
Copyright © 2005 by Blue Mountain Arts, Inc.

Library of Congress Catalog Card Number: 2004018050
ISBN: 0-88396-882-7

Certain trademarks are used under license.
BLUE MOUNTAIN PRESS is registered in U.S. Patent and Trademark Office.

Printed in the United States of America.
First Printing: 2005

❀ This book is printed on recycled paper.

This book is printed on fine quality, laid embossed, 80 lb. paper. This paper has been specially produced to be acid free (neutral pH) and contains no groundwood or unbleached pulp. It conforms with all the requirements of the American National Standards Institute, Inc., so as to ensure that this book will last and be enjoyed by future generations.

Library of Congress Cataloging-in-Publication Data

Josefowitz, Natasha.
    Retirement : wise and witty advice for making it the next great adventure / Natasha Josefowitz.
        p. cm.
        ISBN 0-88396-882-7 (soft cover : alk. paper) 1. Retirees—Life skills guides. 2. Retirement—Planning. I. Title.

    HQ1062.J68 2005
    646.7'9—dc22

                                                            2004018050
                                                            CIP

Blue Mountain Arts, Inc.

P.O. Box 4549, Boulder, Colorado 80306

DEDICATION

To my son, Paul, with all my love and thanks,
for always being there for me,
and whose judgment I value and trust.

ACKNOWLEDGMENTS

As always, I want to thank my secretary, Pamela Morgan, who has typed and re-typed so many of my books. I appreciate her always-appropriate and thoughtful comments.

I thank my editor, Patti Wayant, with whom I have worked on many projects and who is always available, cheerful, and helpful.

I have asked the following people, whose knowledge in the field of aging has greatly contributed to the scope of this book, to read various drafts and to help with revisions of this book. I want to thank Martin Colby, retired General Manager of Channel 6, Fox Television Network; Mike Townsend, Marketing Director of White Sands, a retirement community; J. Adam Milgram, MA, Executive Director of the Sam and Rose Stein Institute for Research on Aging, University of California, San Diego; Dr. Erving Polster, founder and director of the Gestalt Training Center of San Diego and author of *Every Person's Life Is Worth a Novel*; Dr. Calvin Colarusso, Clinical Professor of Psychiatry, University of California at San Diego and author of *Child and Adult Development*; Dr. David Myran, psychiatrist at Baycrest Centre for Geriatric Care, Toronto, Canada; B.J. Curry Spitler, PhD, LCSW, founder of Aging Concerns; and finally, I especially want to thank Herman, my husband and fellow retiree, who is forever helpful, supportive, and loving and with whom I look forward to the next great adventure.

CONTENTS

INTRODUCTION

It is not by muscle, speed, or physical dexterity that great things are achieved, but by reflection, force of character, and judgment; in these qualities old age is usually not poorer, but is even richer.

Marcus Tullius Cicero, 106-43 BC

This book is for all of you in your forties, fifties, and sixties who have aging parents, those of you in your sixties and seventies who are retired or thinking of retirement, and those of you in your eighties and nineties who have "been there and done that."

I am seventy-eight and my husband is eighty. I used to think of myself as middle-aged but now realize that it is my children who are middle-aged. They're all in their fifties with kids in college.

I think of retirement as the next great life-changing adventure. I've had more than a few life-changing experiences, like my first day of school or the day I left home for college or got married or had children or took my first job. All these events signify entering into unknown territories, losing the known and the familiar and going into uncharted waters. Although these waters have been well mapped by others, it is still the great unknown for each individual taking that next step. In other words, we need to reinvent ourselves. Reinventing could be finding new interests, exploring different parts of ourselves, or becoming more of who we already are.

For me, the word retirement means only one thing — control over my time. I can be as busy as I was when I worked full time as a professor of management, but because I don't have to be somewhere from nine to five as most people do, or teach evening classes as I once did, I have freedom. That freedom is the opportunity of choice. I can choose what I want to commit to and for how long. I have taken art classes when I couldn't draw, piano lessons when I couldn't play, and ballroom dancing with a husband who has two left feet. (Arthur Murray, the well-known dance instructor, gave him his money back for being totally hopeless!)

Whatever volunteering I do, I can still take a long trip and not be penalized for my absence. In other words, I can play hooky and not feel guilty, except that I sometimes do. If we go to an afternoon movie, I still feel like I'm doing something wrong, something illicit, which makes it doubly delicious.

This book will look at how to prepare for that next adventure — and how to live it fully, avoiding the pitfalls and celebrating the joys. It's about embracing life before, during, and after the transition.

So start now — smile — you're about to embark on a new adventure!

Just Yesterday

Just yesterday I was still a child
Then quite suddenly I find myself
an old woman

Just a short while ago
my daughter was wearing braces
and ribbons in her hair
When I turned around
she had a PhD

My son walked out the door
in knee socks and short pants
to take the school bus
When he returned
he was wearing a suit
and had a wife and child

My daughter asked me to baby-sit
I was changing a diaper
when my grandson
got up and said he was off to college

Just yesterday my husband
had his first teaching job
Today he's on Social Security and Medicare

Just yesterday
was a short time ago
and suddenly
it is a whole lifetime

CHAPTER 1

Managing the Transition

The Secret of Longevity

When you have learned
what to do and
how to do it well

Look for new things to learn
which at first
you will not do well

You have finished your last day on the job, so what next? The transition is tough — from having a place to go every day to staying home with time on your hands.

Unless you've been let go on a day's notice, you should have planned for this time not only some weeks ago, but months and even years ago. Yet some people spend more time planning a one-week vacation than how they will spend the last third of their lives. Yes, if you live until you're in your nineties and you retire in your sixties, you have one-third more of your life to live. Better give it some thought.

In 1950, the average American retired at age sixty-seven. Today it's sixty-three and falling. In 1900, the average life expectancy was forty-nine. Today men and women who reach sixty-five years of age live to average ages of eighty-one and eighty-four respectively.[1] With life expectancies increasing every year, you could spend a significant portion of your life in retirement.

---

[1] Centers for Disease Control and Prevention.

This is why the preparation is critical. If you do not have a few things you are looking forward to doing after you quit work, and if you have an option, don't quit! If you're not prepared to live without a salary, even if living more modestly, don't stop working unless you have to, and then start looking for another job. If unpaid employment is not your ticket, think again. If you haven't talked to retired friends or researched volunteer possibilities, start immediately. In other words, don't retire *from* something — retire *to* something. Well, you *are* reading this book, that's a start!

My children are the baby boomers everyone is writing about. They are in their early fifties. I have grandchildren in college, and my friends have grandchildren who have graduated and are in the work force. This means that most of my cohorts are thinking of retiring or have already done so. My husband, Herman, and I have retired from full-time teaching. He finally gave up his office at the University of California at San Diego, but I'm still an adjunct professor at San Diego State University.

Work is *outer*-directed with performance as the criteria for reward and other people acting as the judges. This is what the eight-hour workday is all about! Retirement is *inner*-directed, so there is a new need to redefine success, as well as to find happiness in personal life, in relationships, and in creative mental activities. Success means different things to different people. What is it for you? What is important to you now? Is it your own feelings of self-worth or how others perceive you? What will that be predicated on? You are the only one being the judge. The answers will be forthcoming if you ponder these questions.

Although retirement is different for everyone, there are common phases in this process. It can be structured as "planned unemployment" or part-time or full-time employment at another job. Did you know that the Spanish word for retirement is *jubilación*? Sadly, jubilation is not always what many people feel when they finally quit work.

What are your feelings as you contemplate retirement: Jubilation at the idea of sleeping without an alarm clock ticking by your bedside and having time to leisurely read the morning newspaper and do whatever your heart dictates for the rest of the day? Or is it anxiety you feel at the prospect of idle hours and empty days and secret fears of physical or mental disabilities looming in a bleak future?

We trade the biological clock for the mortality one. There is less time to look ahead than there is to look back, so it is even more imperative to make the most of the time we have left. When we were young, we felt like we had endless time ahead of us. Now moments count. We appreciate small pleasures, knowing what we don't do now may not get done. We feel the pressure of time unraveling.

We pose ourselves new questions: What contributions could I still make? What do I still want to learn? What relationships do I want to improve? Who am I?

Identity based on you as a worker is what distinguished you when you were introduced at parties and applied for credit cards. Although you lose that distinguishing mark, you don't lose the need for it. The need for status, satisfaction, friendship, structure, excitement, direction, goals — things usually found through work — must be recognized and alternative sources must be found. Life needs to have meaning and reward as you pass from a life of necessary productivity to one of personal accomplishment, leisure, and choice.

I had an identity crisis when I retired from teaching full time. If I'm not a professor, then who am I? What do I answer when someone asks me, "What do you do?" If I say, "I used to teach," I feel like a "has been." It took me the better part of a year to get over the feeling that I had become less productive, and therefore less significant and less interesting. On top of it all, I was ashamed of feeling that way, as if I should be glad to have more time. I dealt with my feelings by talking about them with my husband and a couple of friends. It helped to find that I was not alone and that others had felt that way, too. And as I became more involved in my community doing volunteer work, the bad feelings started to disappear.

One of the hurdles to overcome after a lifetime of being an expert at work is the need to become a learner again — whether it's a new hobby or skill or just learning how to fill your days meaningfully. This is especially true for people whose main relationships were with people at the workplace. We need to learn to form new relationships and maintain old ones without the glue of job-related topics.

One of the most difficult challenges is finding a passion — and if not a passion, at least something we really love to do and look forward to doing. We don't *grow* old. It's when we stop growing that we *become* old. Happiness in retirement is not a destination, it is a way of traveling, and the prepared person will have a smooth road.

There are three kinds of people: those who make things happen, those to whom things happen, and those who say, "What happened?"

It's up to you to be either the person who makes things happen or the person who can sit back confidently and let things happen. What you decide will be the reward of your next journey — your next adventure.

Getting There Is *All* the Fun!

I have always tried to do it all
to become a better person
to acquire the sufficient knowledge
the necessary skills
the right attitude

And when I have accomplished it
finally made it
or know just about enough
to feel I have arrived

I set my eyes again
on some new, distant goal
working hard
to get to that next
arrival place

So I have come to realize
that it is not the destination
that matters
but the journey

A Little Bit of All or All of a Bit

Not everything
but something
not everyplace
just someplace
not everyone
only someone

If we narrow
our expectations
we can have it all

CHAPTER 2

Looking Ahead

Afraid to Miss Something

I'm glad I went
although it was
totally uninteresting

Had I not gone
I'd never have known
that I would have missed
nothing

I'm planning to retire and live off my savings. I have no idea what I'll do the second day.

Managers become entrepreneurs, salespeople become teachers, and teachers become farmers. Career switching can become an alternate lifestyle or an opportunity to learn new skills. Either way, it is no longer seen as an oddity but as a fact of life and a courageous step to take.

If retirement is on your horizon, you may be looking forward to playing golf and bridge or even sitting in a rocking chair. You're entitled after a life of hard work! But you have other choices, too. You could stay in your old job as a part-time consultant, look for another job in a related field where you can use your current expertise, retrain for a totally different position, start your own business or franchise, or become involved in a volunteer capacity. You can also choose not to be productive in the usual sense, but to embark on a spiritual quest.

Planning ahead while still employed will ease the transition. Think about the times in your life when you were happiest. What were you doing then? Can that be replicated now in some other way? Identify your dreams: what have you always wanted to do but couldn't? What hobbies do you have that could be useful in your new adventure? Do you have an expertise you haven't used? Perhaps you have been collecting antiques. This could land you a job in an auction house or lead you to an international antique market. Not surprisingly, knowledge and skills can often be transferred from one type of work to another. Anyone who has trained workers can train volunteers or work as a teacher's aide. Who you are and what you know are useful no matter what you do, and the more you know and experience, the more you bring to the table next time. Now if this sounds like I'm advocating change for change's sake, I'm not. What I'm advocating is not letting doubts or fears stand in the way.

I taught social work in Switzerland using the case method that I learned at Columbia University. When I moved to the University of New Hampshire, organizational behavior was being taught by the Harvard case method. Using cases was familiar to me and therefore possible, but it was scary at first. I had to adjust from teaching students to become social workers and administrators to teaching them to become good business managers.

If you make a list of everything you've ever done, including volunteer work, and circle all the entries you have most enjoyed, you will see a pattern emerging that you may wish to follow. What part of the newspaper do you read first in the morning? This will give you a clue as to your interests. Ask your friends and family what they think you do best. Go to trade shows, contact professional organizations, study the trade press, and try to meet people in your chosen new field. Contacts are important, and most work is obtained through friends of friends, not the want ads. If your aspirations are at a higher level, consider seeing a headhunter (a person who matches employers to employees). Going back to school, either to learn something new or just for the fun of it, is wonderful. Most universities have continuing education classes. You will make new friends and pursue new interests.

If you want to start your own business, remember that more fail than succeed, due mostly to lack of good business planning and undercapitalization. But whatever you decide to do, one thing is sure, it helps if you are computer literate. I don't mean just word processing, but using graphics programs, e-mail for communication, and the Internet for research purposes.

Starting with the year 2000, 80 percent of all U.S. companies had as many as 30 percent of their employees working outside the traditional workplace, which usually meant working from home with a computer or from the road with a laptop.

If you are homebound or need some extra money, telecommuting may be for you. The advantages are obvious: you control your hours, you don't have to deal with traffic, and you can be there with your family. The downside is loneliness. People miss face-to-face contact. Also, the boundaries between work and home can get blurred. It may be hard to stop work at the end of the day or to keep family matters at bay when working.

Telecommuting is the trend of this new century. Talk to people who are knowledgeable about it. Knowing the advantages and drawbacks will help with decision-making.

The possibilities are there to be investigated. It takes perseverance. With every ending, there is a new beginning, and beginnings spell new challenges. At first there may be many frustrations, but as time goes on, there will be many rewards.

Falling Through the Cracks

I'm often not quite ready
to let go of the past
and so not quite ready
to commit to the future

I'm often
so attached to the old
that I'm not willing
to tackle the new

Some situations are not quite
bad enough to leave
but yet not quite
good enough to stay

However, if I sit too long
between two chairs
I'm in greater danger
of falling right through the crack

CHAPTER 3

Changing Directions

First Times

I wish I never had to do
anything for the first time
It makes me too anxious

I wish I could always start
by doing everything
the second time

Why do some people who have always worked at a secure and steady job suddenly pack up the family and move to a ranch in Montana? Why does the farmer's son leave his land and move to the city and a factory job? Why does someone start a new business on his or her own with all the risks involved? Why these changes of direction?

I know women who have always worked that decide to "drop out" for a while and others who have been community volunteers all their lives that decide to apply for paying jobs. Devoted wives and mothers become career women, while career women leave to spend more time with their families.

Retirement provides an opportunity to change directions and live a new life. It is as if we have a second chance to find out not only what we can do, but who we are — to be someone else. In being laid off or deciding to retire, we can become different in our relationships and environments. On the one hand, we always remain the same core person, but on the other hand, we respond to our environment. If we live in a hostile environment, we become cautious or defensive. If we have supportive people around us, we can allow ourselves to be trusting and to grow and expand our horizons.

Just as we can use the proverbial "mid-life crisis" to make a sharp turnaround, we can use retirement the same way. When daily life is beginning to lose its luster, when we wake up in the morning and sigh with discouragement at the day ahead, when this happens week after week, month after month, then it's time to take a look at what's missing and at what sounds appealing.

Which of your friends or acquaintances do you envy? Whose life do you wish you had? What steps do you need to take to live that life? Are there new skills to acquire or old skills that can be transferred to another application? Are there pleasures that you have postponed? Are there risks to be taken or friends or professionals to consult?

I have changed directions several times in my life and have always felt that it gave me opportunities to live several lives: as a wife and mother, a student at middle age (I got a master's degree at age forty and a PhD at fifty), a clinical social worker, a university professor, and now in my middle seventies, an author and a volunteer. I have lived several lives.

These life changes allowed me not only to move in totally different environments but to respond to these environments as a new person — learning and testing new skills and behaving in ways unfamiliar to me. In other words, one's repertoire gets enlarged and one becomes richer in life experiences. Travel can do this, too, but it's more limited in time and scope, unless of course, you live for a period of time in a different culture.

Yes, there is risk involved. You may leave a bad situation but not find anything better. And yes, staying does afford you the comfort (and discomfort) of the familiar situation and familiar pain. Obviously embarking on a new adventure has no guarantees. Even so, meeting the unknown head on is an opportunity and a challenge that may help you uncover new resources within yourself.

Most people regret what they have not done, what they have missed, the road not taken, the risk avoided. Very few people are sorry that they tried something new, even if they didn't succeed in the way they expected to.

As a people, we seem to strive for competence in whatever we do. Once a high level of competence is achieved, we look for new opportunities to grow and learn. So it's okay to stay put if you're satisfied and okay to move on if you're not.

It is important to remember that you are not making a lifetime commitment to that next activity. You try it, and if you don't like it, you do something else. That's the prerogative of retirement. Too much leisure can become boredom; overdoing can become stress. Too much or too little of anything can create anxiety.

Whether you're forced to retire or decide on your own to call it quits, try your wings and fly away to unknown destinations, meeting new challenges that will need new solutions, but more importantly... new horizons.

Now or Never

I want to live purposefully
aware, cognizant, conscious
of the way I live

I want to have a planned life
thought out, thought through
carefully considered
instead of living from crisis to crisis
responding only to emergencies
taking care of what's most urgent

I don't want to dress in five minutes
gulp down my food in two
be rushed on the phone
type curt e-mails to friends
and run through the house
always late for the next unscheduled event

I want to take time to notice each day
take pleasure in living each hour
I want to enjoy every minute
before it ticks away

CHAPTER 4

Life Explorers

Am I a "Type A" Personality?

I don't plan my life right

I always wish
I were working less
I wish I were less busy
I dream of one lazy day
with nothing to do

Then when such a day —
without deadlines
or bills to pay
or letters to answer
or drawers to clean —
finally happens

I take a walk
read a book
call three friends
eat too much
and wish I had
something to do

Retired people, whether single or married, fall into three main categories:

1. *Outer-Directed*: These are the people who make things happen. They look forward to doing all the things they never had

time for. They are just as busy as before retirement, but without being driven by financial compensation. They may choose to work without pay for nonprofit organizations or they may reinvent themselves and pursue a new interest.

I know someone who upon retiring took on the job of reorganizing a floundering charity organization. It has become a consuming passion. A makeup artist I know is contributing her time to helping people look better after disfiguring accidents when surgery cannot help. Someone else helped set up cultural programs at a local university to help visiting students from foreign countries learn not only our language but also our culture.

2. *Inner-Directed*: These are the people to whom things happen. They have had it with the pressures of work and are looking forward to traveling, a game of golf, meeting friends for lunch, reading books, and taking care of their assets. They are interested in personal growth and may turn to the study of philosophy or religion. If they have grandchildren, spending time with them is a joy, especially for those who never had the time before. It's wonderful for the grandparents and equally great for the grandkids.

A friend of ours who was a CEO all his life started painting and attending poetry workshops, and he loves his new life. Another friend started a book club and enjoys the time he has for reading.

These people may continue this lifestyle forever, but if it begins to wear thin, they may become more outer-directed, while those who make things happen may give up after some years and start becoming more inner-directed. It's also possible to do both: be involved with life on the outside and explore the inner self. Ask yourself questions like these: "What is my purpose in life?" "What legacy do I wish to leave?" "What can I do for the betterment of humankind or, if not for humankind, for my neighbor?"

3.   *Undirected*: These are the people who ask, "What happened?" They have either been forced into retirement by a mandatory age requirement, downsizings, mergers, or poor health, or they have chosen to retire without much thought as to how to manage their lives. Sudden retirement may be quite traumatic. The undirected are unprepared and have to play catch-up quickly. With nothing to do and nowhere to go, they are often restless and sometimes even depressed. Seeing a healthcare professional may help with the transition. It's never too late to start preparing, but the transition is tough.

A former office manager I know was in this situation. He quit work quite suddenly with no clue as to how he would fill his days. His wife complained about having to fix lunch and be a companion when she had a busy life of her own. He tried volunteering in a hospital, but on the first day he was asked to make coffee and carry trays. Having never made coffee in his life, he quit. He wanted to teach but had no experience in the classroom. He used to play tennis but wasn't fit enough anymore. He didn't know what to do with himself and became depressed, which in itself was paralyzing. He listened to all the suggestions his friends made but didn't act on any of them. He finally agreed to see a doctor and is being helped with anti-depressants and discussions about finding a new life focus.

What could he have done to prevent this sad outcome? Prepare!

What can he do now? Look for a new business venture, become employed in a business where he can work less than full time, find a philanthropic organization where he can work on a committee, and read the next chapter on volunteering.

If you take a class in photography and this becomes a passion where you go on photo shoots and learn to develop your own film, you are outer-directed. If you take a class in photography and are enjoying taking pictures of the grandkids but not much else, then you are inner-directed. If you take that class in photography just to fill up the time and it bores you, but you don't quit because it's something to do, you are among the undirected. You will remain that way until you quit that class and enroll in something better suited to your inclination. Most universities offer a variety of continuing education classes. Community colleges often have free computer classes as well as other offerings. Having a spouse, friend, or family member sort out the information and help with the choices can sometimes make the difference to a reluctant retiree. Keep searching until you hit on that "just-right" activity or project.

One of the first things you should do is call your community senior citizen center where people gather for all types of activities, including lectures on a variety of topics. These centers are a wonderful resource for all kinds of senior needs.

Having children at close proximity is a great help, too. Ours are in England, Canada, the East Coast, and the Northwest, and we live in San Diego. Even though our kids all offered to have us live with them when the time comes that we no longer can be independent, this is not an option I would accept. I might, however, consider living near them.

If my husband and I are no longer able to stay in our home or we become widowed or disabled, then we want to go to a retirement community with assisted living and nursing care. Getting your name on a waiting list, though it will likely require putting some money down, may be a good idea because these facilities are filled with aging baby boomers' parents and eventually with the baby boomers themselves.

We have made verbal contracts with several of our older friends to look in on each other and hold each other's hands if necessary, but it is also important to have young friends who can help out when needed.

I'm Not Climbing Ladders Anymore

I have discovered the joy of caring less
about success
about visibility and significance
about what others think of me
about how I sound

I have given up on rinses for gray hair
on the creams that don't help wrinkles
I have finally accepted
that those extra pounds
will probably be part of me forever
I notice less the possible slights
I can overlook being overlooked

I do not need to see all the sights when I travel
If I miss a cathedral or a museum
it is not the end of the world
I don't have to go to every good movie
or read the books on the bestseller lists

I'm not climbing any ladders
I'm not fighting for center stage
I'm not competing for any favors
I don't owe anyone anything

And as I watch others
fight for a place in the sun
I can sit peacefully in the twilight
doing my needlepoint
enjoying a quiet talk
with a big mug of hot tea

CHAPTER 5

Volunteering

Important Words

*The least important words
are "I" or "me"
The more important word
is "you"
But the most important word of all
is a combination of the first two
"we"*

We all have a basic need to contribute: to give, not just to receive. Volunteering is one way to do this, but it is also work. Sometimes it's working just as hard as when you were employed, except that you like what you do, you can stop when you want to, and you don't get paid.

So how can you volunteer and why? There are two ways to do it: by giving money or by giving time.

Giving a significant amount of money is possible for a very few privileged people, and then the questions always are: how much and to whom? How much you give will depend not only on how much you earn, but also on how much you spend. Some people have dependents, such as children or aging parents, large mortgages, or they are living on a fixed income. Others may have a steady source of income that will increase over time and no major responsibilities. Retirees in either scenario, while perhaps having access to the same dollar amount, need to calculate their spending very differently.

Should you give to one or two organizations or spread the giving among many? This depends on whether your heart leans toward a specific cause or whether you tend to respond to friends' requests for donations to their favorite charities. Larger amounts to one or two charities are more visible than a few dollars to many organizations.

By identifying yourself with a specific cause, one you believe in, you will be working with people who share your interests. Sitting on boards, joining committees, and doing fundraising for a charitable cause can be most rewarding. Board membership can open many doors because you get to know people who are both interesting and influential in your community.

Volunteering time can mean anything from working in a shelter or a political organization, delivering food, mentoring a child, or reading in a school, to licking envelopes, soliciting door-to-door, or making speeches. Are you interested in environmental issues, in education, in healthcare? Do you want to mentor a homeless child or work in a senior center? Choose organizations that mirror your own interests.

Research on volunteer work has shown that people who never do charity work are 2.25 times more likely to die prematurely than those who volunteer at least once a week. Researchers at the University of Michigan discovered a remarkable link between volunteer work and longevity by surveying 1,211 adults over sixty-five (mostly retirees) in 1986 and checking up on them eight years later. The subjects who volunteered at least forty hours each year to a single cause were 40 percent more likely than non-volunteers to be alive at the end of the study. The trend held even when researchers took differences in the two groups' incomes, health, and number of weekly social interactions into account. Interestingly, focusing on a single cause seemed to be crucial. Volunteers who spread their time among several organizations did not gain an advantage in longevity.

Whatever your reasons for volunteering, whether it is a worthy cause you believe in or you want the added benefit of visibility or social status, the result will be of great value to some charitable organization, and you will become a generous person with an enhanced immune system. What a deal!

The following national organizations recruit older volunteers: Administration on Aging, United Way, Elderhostel, and Senior Corps.

Contact information for organizations mentioned in this chapter:

- Administration on Aging: www.aoa.gov; 202-619-0724

- United Way: 701 North Fairfax St., Alexandria, VA 22314; www.unitedway.org; 703-836-7112

- Elderhostel: www.elderhostel.org; 877-426-8056

- Senior Corps: www.seniorcorps.org; 800-424-8867

Post-Retirement Crisis

No alarm clocks
no gulped-down coffee
not stuck in traffic afraid to be late
no preparations for a lecture
no office hours
no student papers to grade

I have retired
from full-time teaching
I am retired
from my identity
What will replace my useful days?
How will I fill the empty hours?
So I joined five boards
became a member
of two service clubs
learned to draw by
using the right side of my brain
and volunteered
at my local hospital
I joined a book club
took piano lessons
attended classes on nutrition
went to lectures
on the latest brain research
subscribed to four medical journals
and became more frantic
than I was before

I'm having a
post-retirement crisis!

CHAPTER 6

He's Ready to Retire, but She Wants to Continue Working

False Expectations

A woman marries a man expecting that he will change but he doesn't

A man marries a woman expecting that she won't change and she does

We hear a lot about dual-career couples and how they manage their responsibilities at home when both work full time. We also read a great deal about the conflicts women experience juggling children and a career, but there is very little written about the couple who is thinking about retirement.

If she has been a full-time housewife and he retires, this can be their golden years of new-shared interests, travel, family, and hobbies, or it can also be that he's bored and she feels he's always underfoot. In other words: for better, for worse, but not for lunch.

It is very difficult to function without a schedule when, for fifty years, one was set for you. It is important for people who have worked all their lives to continue with regular activities — be it gardening, politics, board memberships, community volunteering, reading, or anything else that provides satisfaction. For most people, having a routine after retirement provides needed structure.

But there is a new problem emerging. What if both the husband and wife have worked full time? He may be ready to retire, and she may be in the midst of her most productive years. Or what if one or both of them has started on a new career after the children have grown? After having stayed home, she may be looking outward, whereas after having been out there, he may be looking inward toward home and family.

A recent study showed that 25 percent of women retire at the same time as their husbands, 44 percent retire before their husbands, and 30 percent do so after.

It is within the last category that difficulties can emerge. Because women are often younger than their husbands and many started to work later in life, the decision to stay in the job market may be an economic one, based on the need to accrue a good pension and bigger Social Security benefits. Also, while he may feel burned out and glad to be away from the daily pressures of work, she may be at the crossroads of her greatest opportunities.

He has a legitimate wish to be able to share his retirement years with his lifelong companion, while she has an equally legitimate wish to be able to fulfill herself.

Couples need to start thinking about this dilemma before it is upon them. Will he be satisfied to shop and cook while she's at work? Will he be lonely or will he enjoy this time on his own? Will she feel guilty about the role reversal? Will she feel like she's abandoning him?

Couples must be clear about their expectations and needs, and negotiate the compromises they can live with. If this is discussed ahead of time, he may want to arrange for a consulting job or volunteer activity after his retirement, or she may prepare herself for part-time work. They may also decide that if he stops working and she doesn't, they will manage their time together around weekends, with the husband sharing housekeeping responsibilities.

It is interesting to note that men often have a harder time adjusting to being at home than women. That's because most men are used to being gone all day, so they don't know what to do with themselves at home. Without their jobs, they have lost their purpose. On top of that, they probably have not formed close friendships outside of work, so they don't have anyone with whom to go to lunch, attend a sporting event, play a game of golf, take a walk, or just have a chat.

One suggestion is to form a group of other retirees and meet on a regular basis. A friend of ours who retired from a job where he wielded a great deal of influence was lost without the friends he had made at work. No longer able to provide the people he knew with the perks of his position, such as tickets to theater openings, after-concert receptions, or VIP tours of studios, he felt he did not have much to offer. Being a lovable guy and wanting friendship, he was at a loss.

So he asked my husband to help him start a group of men over seventy to meet monthly at each other's homes for coffee and dessert. They have been doing this since 1996, and some of them also see each other in between. They have all become close friends and support one another when problems occur. In fact, the wife of one of the men died this year, and every day a member of the group calls and takes the newly widowed man out for lunch or includes him in a family event. Their group discussions vary from health problems, such as coping with diminished capacities, to relationships with grown children and grandchildren, to money issues, to the latest movie or good book, but mostly they center around the value of friendship and how to remain both interested and interesting.

One of our friends has a daily breakfast meeting with a group of other retirees at a local coffee house where they talk mostly about politics. Another meets weekly with his buddies to share the latest jokes.

If forming such a group is of interest to you, invite a couple of men to join you and ask each one to bring a friend or two who might also be interested in joining. Everyone has to be committed to meeting regularly or it won't work.

When older women are divorced or widowed, there are few if any available men, and if the children don't live close by, loneliness can be a big problem. It is difficult for an older woman to go alone to a restaurant, a movie, or an artistic event. Parking in dark, underground structures, using stairwells, or even taking elevators may be dangerous. What some of my friends have done is start a group of widowed or divorced women who meet regularly to exercise, have lunch, go to a concert, and generally support one another in times of trouble. Many don't drive anymore, but there are usually some who still do. I can imagine that when the time comes, they could give up owning individual cars, hire a college student to drive, and still go everywhere they want to go.

The important thing to remember is that there are possible solutions to keep from remaining alone and sedentary. Pending retirement is a time for honest reappraisal of your life goals, realistically looking at your past achievements, and accomplishing what has been set aside in pursuit of a livelihood. It is no easy task, but it may be the most rewarding time of a person's life.

Growing Pains

Older women
with kids grown up
are finally free to realize
long-delayed dreams

Women are turning outward

Older men
with dreams fulfilled or forgotten
are ready to take
time for themselves
and time for their families

Men are turning inward

Measuring Success

It used to be
that a man's success
was measured by the fact
that his wife
could stay home
and not have to work

Today, a woman's success
is measured by the fact
that she can have a career
and not have to stay home

How is today's man
living with yesterday's values
to measure his success?

CHAPTER 7

To Move or Not to Move – That Is the Question

Someone from Back Home

A familiar face
in an unfamiliar place
even if it's someone
I don't know very well
I rush smiling and hugging
I've found a friend
in a familiar face
I'm not alone
in the unfamiliar place

You're about to retire! With the children gone and the dog having died of old age, should you move out of your house that's now too large? Should you move to smaller quarters, to a warmer climate, nearer the children, or into a retirement community with independent living and assisted-care facilities in case the need arises?

These are questions we all face at that time of life when work does not require us to be in a specific location. We are free to choose where the rest of our lives will unfold.

When my husband got early retirement at the University of New Hampshire, we decided to move to California and escape the six months of cold weather, but we did it early enough so that we could still become part of the working community. I joined the faculty of San Diego State University's School of Business, and he joined the faculty of the University of California at San Diego. Many years later, after having established active professional lives, we retired with active social lives, surrounded by many friends and colleagues.

The decision to move or not to move is not an easy process. There are many concerns. Will you have to move eventually because of too many stairs in your house or no public transportation close by? Maybe you are too isolated from family and friends or have an older home with too much upkeep. If a cold climate keeps you indoors many months of the year, you might want to consider moving to a gated community in one of the warmer states. Moving nearer to your children is another option many people choose. Making the move sooner rather than later allows you to make new friends and participate in a lifestyle of your choosing. Then if you ever become widowed or move into a long-term care facility, you will have friends and family there who will visit and give you support.

Or maybe you're just tired of running a household, with all the cooking, cleaning, and annoying little things that always need to be fixed. My husband is pretty good at rewiring and plumbing problems, but a week does not go by that the house does not require another fix. Just last week, our washing machine conked out, the TV wire got frayed and had to be replaced, the bathroom faucet sprung a leak, and a swarm of bees decided to settle in a corner of the roof. This meant four different service calls and staying home waiting for the people to show up. (It's also called the joys of ownership!)

Still, many people prefer staying in their familiar surroundings, but need help with everyday tasks. The National Association of Professional Geriatric Care Managers is committed to keeping older people in their homes. They offer help with meals, transportation, nursing care, and even provide companions.

With the aging population growing larger every year, it is smart to think ahead to a time when living alone will not be an option. If a retirement community with assisted living as well as skilled nursing care is a possibility, even if in the far future, it is a good idea to put down a small reservation deposit to ensure that if and when the time comes, you will be high on the priority list. For some of these places, there is a two-year or longer waiting list. We are not growing stronger and more able as we age, and eventually even holding our own may not be easy. Thinking ahead does not mean an inevitable move; it is an insurance policy like any other.

Gather information about facilities in your desired location from doctors, social workers, and resources, such as Eldercare Locator or your local office on aging.

If you're going to move "someday," it is better to do it earlier rather than later. Energy levels drop every year. It's easier to do the horrendous job of downsizing while you're still able to look through your books, tapes, clothes, files, and kitchen utensils and not have someone else do the giving away or throwing out for you because you've become too weak or too overwhelmed to do it yourself.

Like most people, we have too much stuff. I vow every day to start getting rid of some of it. We gave away a lot of clothes and books, but it did not make a dent. "Stuff" is the bane of my life. Objects are everywhere — on tabletops, on shelves, in drawers. They are souvenirs of things acquired in exotic places or given to us by friends. How can I divest myself of all these memories? Memories are part of us, and by giving away an object, we lose the memory attached to it. This can be so painful that many of us hold on to things we no longer use for far too long. I plan to take photographs of my most loved objects that I know I will have to get rid of.

The options are there. We are free to choose, yet we can be paralyzed by that freedom. There is no need to rush into a choice; we just need to let it percolate in the back of our minds. This choice becomes more pressing with the death of a spouse. Where will the newly single person live? To make a decision while under the stress of mourning is a bad idea. Moving in with children may sound good at the moment, but how will that work out in the long run? Healthcare professionals suggest deferring major decisions for one year after the death of a spouse. Staying in one's home and renting out a room so as to not be alone is one option. Another is to share a housekeeper with friends. It is important to have someone supervise the care of the person living alone. You do not need to think alone. It is okay to obsess and talk as often as necessary with as many people as are willing to listen. You can never be totally sure that the particular decision is the right one for the long run, but "almost sure" is pretty good. Then if it doesn't work out, there are other options. We are not married to our decisions.

If moving and downsizing is the decision, the question is: what to do with the accumulations of a lifetime? Hopefully the kids will want some of it. My kids didn't, so I'm waiting for the grandkids to grow up and want it. I'm not hopeful.

So the books will go to schools in less developed countries, the clothes (I have enough for three lifetimes because I never throw anything out) will go to charity, and the kitchen gadgets will go to a garage sale. The collection of bric-a-brac will go to friends as birthday gifts, and I'll have the added pleasure of being able to enjoy their delight at receiving something I have treasured.

CAN'T DECIDE?

In considering a retirement community, one of the major factors is timing. When should you make such a move? When residents of a retirement community were asked about their experiences, many felt there were significant benefits to relocating *sooner* — rather than later. Some of the important advantages are:

You are better able to handle the mental and physical requirements of the move, such as selling your present home, disposing of unnecessary furniture, and the actual move and relocation.

You can make the move at a time of your own choosing, rather than being forced by unexpected conditions, such as illness or the loss of a spouse.

You will be in a better position to make friends with the other residents and will have a longer time to enhance and enjoy these new friendships.

You will be in better physical condition, more active, and mobile, so if you are moving to another area, you'll be able to familiarize yourself with the area's many attractions.

You will save financially because, historically, entrance fees increase regularly.

You will avoid the risk of waiting too long and someday not qualifying, physically and mentally, to move into an independent living facility.

You will experience the luxury and independence of "catered living." Household chores will be reduced dramatically, and you'll have time for the things you've always wanted to do.

You will relieve yourself of the burden of managing a lifelong collection of "things" and be able to focus on those possessions that are most precious to you.

You can relieve any pressures family or friends may feel in wanting to ensure that your retirement life is safe, secure, and invigorating.

Considering all the foregoing, the retirement community residents that were queried said, "Why wait?"

Contact information for organizations mentioned in this chapter:

- The National Association of Professional Geriatric Care Managers: 1604 North Country Club Road, Tucson, Arizona 85716-3102; www.caremanager.org; 520-881-8008

- Eldercare Locator: www.eldercare.gov; 800-677-1116

The Grass Is Always Greener

When I'm hot in the summer
I dream of winter's snow
When I'm cold in the winter
I long for summer's warmth

When I was a child
I wanted to be grown up
When I was twenty
I wished to be older
When I was middle-aged
I wanted to be twenty
When I reached retirement
I wished to be middle-aged

And so I went through life
never having what I wanted
instead of delighting in what I had

And now that I'm much older
I have learned to savor
each moment
and have no regrets
over what might have been

CHAPTER 8

Controlled by Clutter

Our Lady of Perpetual Fatigue

*The patron saint of women is
Our Lady of Perpetual Fatigue,
for we are bound by
responsibility, commitment,
duty, and expectations.
We are role-bound to behave as
good wives, mothers, daughters,
workers, neighbors, friends,
community volunteers.*

*We must provide and produce,
give much, take little,
be there, get involved,
act selfless and courageous,
using ourselves until used up,
praying to Our Lady of Perpetual Fatigue
for one quiet day
with no obligations —
one day with no guilt —
just one day to ourselves.*

If you are the average American, you are overweight, stuck in traffic for countless hours, and have mounting debt on your multiple credit cards. Your home is cluttered, your car is a gas-guzzler, and you own electronic gadgets you not only have not learned to use but have given up trying, except for the most basic capacity of that technology.

You own too much stuff and are also owned by it. While you decry having too many possessions, you keep adding more to them with impulse buying, like that not-needed gadget in the hardware store or the gift you bought Aunt Minnie while on some exotic cruise, except that Aunt Minnie didn't want it, so now it's on your shelf.

There is a new counter-trend called "voluntary simplicity" to slow luxury living and spending and its negative fallout. It can mean different things to different people: from not buying the giant TV screen to curtailing computer games for the children in favor of reading a book. My house does not need another gift, and I have enough clothes for the rest of my life. But when retirement looms nearer, it is a wonderful time to reassess the way we live and make the necessary changes. Retirement can be a time of reappraisal, of simplification, of doing what we always believed in but never had the time to pursue, such as spending more time with family, learning new skills, taking adult education classes, or volunteering. Our communities need us wiser folks.

I believe in voluntary simplicity. My life is often out of control. By this I mean there is more to do than time to do it, and I end up frantic about what's left undone.

My stack of magazines that I plan to read someday is getting higher, my file drawers are getting tighter, the photos in shoeboxes are overflowing, and I can't find the top of my desk. I keep looking at the same papers with anxiety, not knowing where to file them and yet unable to toss them away. There are days that my overflowing desktop ends up on the dining room table, which then gets swept up in an undifferentiated pile when guests are about to arrive.

We were supposed to have fewer papers with the advent of computers, but I often print out my files for fear of losing them or not finding them when I need them. So that didn't work. I spend countless minutes a day opening junk mail or looking for papers that are lost on my desktop. Paper management skills should be taught in high schools and colleges.

I have several types of piles of papers. The largest is the do-it-later pile, which keeps growing with everything from newspaper clippings to business cards to brochures to take-out menus to invitations I'm not sure I want to accept. This often becomes the "I-don't-know-what-to-do-with-this" pile. These are the papers I can't decide whether to file (someone might need them someday) or to toss (they're too good to throw away).

But this isn't just about papers. It is also about books. Even though I know I will never reread most of them, I loved some of them or the author signed them or maybe a friend or my grandkids will want to read them.

It's about clothes. If they don't fit now, they will when I lose weight. Then there is that expensive suit that I hardly wore and the outmoded dress that just might become fashionable again.

It's about the kitchen utensils. I haven't used some of them in years, but they sit in drawers ever ready for that special recipe for which they will be needed. It has not happened yet!

Should I mention my award-winning college papers, my university teaching notes, cards from birthdays past, articles I have written that are now irrelevant, or clippings of wondrous, never-tried recipes that are in the attic? I still have my children's certificates showing they passed their first swimming lessons.

So I have learned to ask myself five questions for every piece of paper that comes my way:

1. What category does this fit into: urgent, to read, to do, to file?

2. Why would I want to keep it? (Have a good answer ready.)

3. When would I ever need it? (If not soon, toss it.)

4. Where would I look for it? (This is important. I have a miscellaneous file that I never look at. Bad idea!)

5. Where else is this information available?

Answering these questions helps, but if and when you decide to move to a smaller house, smaller apartment, or retirement home, you will have to be even more disciplined about downsizing. For every "thing" you own, you'll have to ask yourself:

1. How long has it been since I wore it, used it, looked at it? If it's more than a couple of years, give it away.

2. Do I have a good rationale for keeping it and not just a vague feeling?

3. Do I have a friend who might enjoy having it?

4. Is it an item I can bring to a charity benefit?

In the end, if you still want to hold on to your useless, obsolete, not-needed-in-the-foreseeable-future object, then by all means, do so. It is now by definition: your treasure!

I find it easier to give something to a family member or friend than to sell it, give it to charity, or throw it out. But then I run into the problem of my kids not wanting my stuff, because they have too much of their own. So I ask myself: who will appreciate that African sculpture, that Indian shawl, those beads from an exotic island, the name of which I don't remember, and the other travel souvenirs that have meaning only to me? Yet it must be done.

I have figured out a way: Completely furnish that next residence with whatever fits from your old home, including furniture, art, books, and clothes. Then with whatever is left over that the children don't want, have a party and give it away to your friends, call in an estate appraiser and have everything carted off, or call Goodwill or the Salvation Army and have them pick up the rest.

Either we allow our possessions and our care of them to control us or we take control of the clutter in our lives. The tough part is the parting of the ways, but once the objects are out of sight, they will be out of mind and not missed. That's what I'm told by recent retirees who have moved to smaller quarters.

The Storeroom

Every January first
we vow to clean up the storeroom
We plan to open all those boxes
that never got unpacked
in twenty years and many moves
Until one day I said to my husband
"Either we move to a bigger house
or we clean out the storeroom"
So we set aside two weekends
rolled up our sleeves
and did the deed

There were boxes on top of boxes
shelves filled with things we'll never use
scarves and mittens
hardened ski wax
rusted batteries inside of toys
a coffee maker, an ice bucket
paper plates from parties past
out-of-style hats
an old fur blanket
children's books and roller skates
my son's soap sculptures from kindergarten
my daughter's drawings from first grade
mountain boots, some empty frames
a jigsaw puzzle with missing pieces

As we sort through a lifetime of objects
memories tumble out, too
Some make us smile as we remember
Some tug and hurt as we discard
Then everything goes back into boxes
most labeled "For donation"
and stacked again
but in the driveway
not in the storeroom
which now stands empty
of memories

CHAPTER 9

Healthy, Wealthy, and Wise

Every day, take a multivitamin
the one for seniors
plus calcium for your bones
magnesium to help absorption
and vitamin D if you don't go out in the sun
Eat less red meat and more fish
My mother called it "brain food"
Surprisingly, she was right

Add color to your diet
yellow vegetables, like squash
orange for carrots
dark green for spinach or kale —
the darker green, the better
so romaine and not iceberg lettuce —
red like berries and tomatoes
blue for blueberries —
they are the best antioxidants —
white for garlic, onions, and celery
Add cruciferous vegetables
like broccoli and cauliflower
citrus fruits like oranges
bananas for potassium
One ounce of nuts is good
more is too fattening
Use olive oil or canola oil
Eat grains like brown rice and whole wheat bread
Go easy on sugar, salt, and fat
Only one bite of dessert
Okay, maybe two
and one small piece of chocolate
only if you have followed the above advice

Do this and you'll be healthy —
don't know about wealthy
but certainly wise

Are you taking your vitamins? Do you exercise regularly? Do you pay attention to the foods you eat and try to make healthful choices? Are you at a good weight? Do you put sunscreen on when you go out? Do you have fun?

I hope you answered "yes" to all of the above. I'm pretty good at making healthy choices, except for chocolate.

So let's start with vitamins. As we grow older, our stomachs don't have enough gastric acid to absorb all the nutrients we need. For that reason, you should take a multivitamin made for seniors that has less iron.[1]

Take calcium. You can get some calcium from dairy products and dark, leafy vegetables, but that's not enough. So take a supplement, but add magnesium for better absorption. Vitamin D needs also go up after age seventy, especially if you don't get enough sun. I also take extra C, E, and a B complex. Before taking anything beyond a multivitamin, you should check with your doctor. Women, especially, should get a bone-density test to check for osteoporosis.

I hope you eat lots of vegetables and fruits and whole grains and go easy on red meat. Fish is good and so are nonfat dairy products. I use olive or canola oil. Remember to drink enough water. As we age, our thirst signals get weaker.[2] I don't like water, so I make iced, decaf green tea and sip that throughout the day. Eat by color, and the darker the better: dark green, red, orange, yellow, and blue fruits and vegetables; brown for grains; less white bread, white pasta, or white rice. Also eat less sugar and less fat. I promise myself every day to abstain from cookies and candies, and most days I do.

---

[1] *Tufts University Health and Nutrition Letter* 20, no. 2 (April 2002).

[2] Ibid.

Yes, I put on sunscreen every morning — even on a rainy day. It becomes routine. So do I have fewer wrinkles? Don't ask. That's not why I use it; it's to protect against skin cancer. Get a yearly checkup, and be sure to include your vaccinations: tetanus every ten years, pneumonia vaccine once after age sixty-five, and flu vaccine every fall.

I mentioned fun. That is so important for optimum health. Laughter acts as a stress reducer, lowers blood pressure, boosts your immune system, increases your circulation, and can act as a painkiller. So tell jokes, see funny movies, have a good time with friends, read a good book, and do whatever else gives you pleasure. If you smile, your brain thinks something nice is happening and sends out the good hormones. So smile — or at least pretend to smile — because the brain believes your face.

In a survey by AARP, approximately one-third of Americans age fifty-five and older said that the older they get, the more fun they have, one-third said they have less fun, and one-third have about the same amount.[3]

So how to be in that first third? It's a matter of attitude. Make fun a priority and always try to learn new things.

Play! It increases creativity, which is one of the signs of living successfully. Creativity helps your mind, and the more fun people have, the better they rate their physical health. In fact, Yale University researchers found that positive attitudes about old age are more important than wealth, gender, and even cholesterol levels for adding years to your life — seven and a half years longer, to be precise.[4] In other words, think positively and live longer.

---

[3] Priscilla Grant, *AARP Modern Maturity* (July/August 2002).

[4] Levy, et al., "Longevity Increased by Positive Self-Perception of Aging," *Journal of Personality and Social Psychology* 83 (August 2002): 261-270.

In a study of 660 people going back nearly twenty-five years, researchers compared their responses to statements, such as "Things keep getting worse as I get older," with their mortality rates. People who strongly rejected such notions lived a lot longer. Lead researcher Becca Levy believes that these people were able to "internalize" a positive image of aging, despite society's negative stereotypes, and somehow a psychological connection was forged between that image and the will to live.[5]

Also, senior citizens who own pets are less likely to be depressed, better able to tolerate social isolation, and more active than those who do not own pets.[6] My new dog, Molly, takes me on a walk twice a day, whether I feel like it or not, and keeps me moving. Pets depend on us, whereas family members may not, and it's good to feel needed. Also pets don't expect to be named in your will.

Our cat is from the county animal shelter. Our dog Tessa was from the Humane Society. She was fourteen years old, and we had her from puppyhood. At the end of her life, she was seventy-five pounds, and I could no longer lift her when she was unable to jump into the car. She also didn't see or hear as well as she used to. I sometimes felt a lot like her. But she still enjoyed our homecomings, a little piece of chicken from our plate, and singing with us. Actually the three of us howled in a bonding ceremony every morning.

Tessa was a "senior citizen" who had slowed down a bit but still had perky moments, enjoyed life, and earned her keep as a watchdog (the intruder had to be loud enough). She didn't have any financial worries. By the year 2005, thirty-five million

---

[5] Marianne Szegedy-Maszak, "Good Old Thoughts," *US News and World Report* (August 5, 2002).

[6] "Live Longer and Better," *Mayo Clinic Proceedings* (1998).

Americans will be sixty-five years or older, and for them, the financial aspect of retirement is critical.

Don't make the mistake of underestimating the impact of inflation. You can't know what it will be in ten years. Moreover, the cost of drugs and services may rise even faster than inflation. This means that you may have to think of saving more than you might have originally planned. It isn't only how much you save and how you will manage your money, but also how you plan to withdraw your assets and spend them.

Use a financial adviser to help you project how much money you will need to live on. Get information about health insurance and long-term care insurance.

Chocolate Is Not
an Endangered Species

*I keep forgetting that
chocolate is not an
endangered species
and therefore
I will not lose
my only chance
to eat it
at the moment
it happens to be available*

Daily Dilemmas

*If I order a soft drink
I get the sugar
calories and cavities*

*If I choose a diet drink
I get chemicals
and a chance at cancer*

*I'm not always sure
whether I'd rather
die young but thin
or old and fat*

CHAPTER 10

You *Can* Teach an Old Dog New Tricks

Older Is Better

Older is wiser
It does not fret over little things
has no small children to worry about
has adjusted well to a mate
or to life without one
can pursue interests postponed in youth
has new leisure with new hobbies

Older is easier
It does not have to impress
anyone anymore
is asked advice
is given seats on buses
is respected and sought after
does not worry about face-lifts
or dyeing gray hair

Older is an arrival place
where there is time for passion
and time for contemplation
and time to enjoy time

When I told my doctor I felt like a spring chicken, he said I was really more like an old hen. I suppose most of you who are reading this book are not spring chickens any more, but mature birds — so let's talk about aging.

1. *The Senses*: Although normal aging may somewhat affect taste and smell, you can still appreciate a good meal. There may be some hearing loss, but you can do something to halt further decline. Protect your ears from loud noises; anything loud enough to hurt your ears can lead to permanent damage. I hate to think of all our grandchildren who listen to terribly loud music. They will all be deaf by my age!

Eyesight should be checked regularly, and recent studies have shown that some vitamin combinations can prevent or slow macular degeneration, the leading cause of blindness in older people.

2. *Sleep Needs*: Did you know that compared to the past thirty years, women are working two hundred hours more a year and men one hundred hours more? In the United States, we are all taking fewer vacation days than we did even ten years ago. We get less sleep and are becoming a sleep-deprived nation.

The need for sleep does not decline with age, but some medications may interfere with sleep as well as needing to get up and go to the bathroom during the night. I don't drink anything past 6 p.m. Also, eating dinner earlier rather than later reduces stomach acid, which is important for people who have heartburn.

3. *Sex*: It can be as good as ever, given the opportunity, which is just a little less frequent. Antidepressants and high blood pressure medications can impair libido, as can overuse of alcohol and unusual stress. Many retirement communities no longer frown on sex between their older, consenting adults.

4. *Exercise*: Even if it's not strenuous, exercise is beneficial for most people. Those who do aerobic activities and strength

training are most likely to be able to live independently. Of course, intense exercise for a ninety-year-old is different from a fifty-year-old, which is different from a twenty-year-old. To remain flexible, you also have to stretch every day. If you decide to buy some weights or go to a gym to lift, be sure to have a professional trainer show you how to use them correctly. Walk at least five days a week, and exercise at least three times. You need all three: aerobic exercise for your heart, strength training for your muscles and bones, and flexibility to avoid falls. This is the most important thing you can do for yourself. I know it can be boring, so do it with a friend. If you are in poor health, you can still exercise sitting in a chair. Just do it!

5. *Pain Relief*: Being old and sick does not mean having to endure pain. If your doctor does not give you enough medication for pain relief, write to the American Board of Pain Medicine for a list of doctors who are certified pain specialists.

6. *Mental Functioning*: Older people are better learners due to their larger vocabulary, broader life experiences, and wider perspective. It may, however, take an older person a longer time to retrieve a piece of information. Yes, there is a slower reaction time, but aging does not have to affect cognitive and mental functioning. I often feel that I'm wiser than ever and able to understand life's little nuances more clearly, yet sometimes I can't think of a common word I use every day and have to substitute another one. Alas... I often need to learn again what I already know.

A lifetime of experiences does give us more wisdom. We've "been there, done that," so now we really do know better!

Our brains' mantra is "use it or lose it," like any muscle in our bodies. It is critical to participate in book clubs, Elderhostel programs, attend classes, and learn new things. We should do whatever it takes to exercise our brains, which, by the way, can still grow new synapses until the day we die. Those of us who stay mentally active have less risk for dementia and memory loss. I have started to do crossword puzzles and plan to learn bridge after I finish the next two books I'm working on.

Remember: it's only when you're "over the hill" that you can begin to pick up speed.

Contact information for organizations mentioned in this chapter:

- American Board of Pain Medicine: 4700 W. Lake Avenue, Glenview, IL 60025; www.abpm.org; 847-375-4726

- Elderhostel: 11 Avenue de Lafayette, Boston, MA 02111; www.elderhostel.org; 877-426-8056

Stages

Reaching 20
was saying goodbye
to childlike behavior
and worrying about being grown-up

Arriving at 30
was experiencing parenthood
and worrying about new responsibilities

Getting to 40
was wondering if this was where I was going
and worrying about the midlife crisis

Passing 50
was entering middle age
and worrying about wrinkles and gray hair

Becoming 60
was enjoying grandchildren
and worrying about when to retire

Attaining 70
was pursuing new interests
and worrying about aging family members

Achieving 80
was celebrating advancing age
and worrying about one's health

And finally embracing 90
was being delighted at still being around
and not worrying about anything anymore

CHAPTER 11

Is It Alzheimer's or Old-Timers?

Young people don't worry when
they don't remember
their best friend's name
lose their car keys twice a week
can't find their wallets
misplace their glasses
walk into a room
and not know what it was
they were looking for
forget their own phone numbers
can't think of a common word
they use every day
can't recall what they just said
lose the list of things to remember

Young people just shrug
their shoulders
but older people think
they have Alzheimer's Disease

The fear of potential mental deterioration is with us more and more as we age, and looking after a person with dementia is one of the most taxing responsibilities ever.

Today over four million people suffer from Alzheimer's Disease (AD). It strikes nearly one in twenty people at age seventy, and one in five who live to age eighty will have the disease. It is one of the major causes of disability in the older population in the U.S. today.

So when I look for my hat everywhere and find it on my head, I get upset with myself. When my husband asks me the same question three times, I worry. When I can't find the piece of paper that was in my hand one minute ago, I get frantic. When I forget what I was about to say or can't remember whom I'm calling by the time she answers the phone, I think I have Alzheimer's, and if not me, then my husband thinks he has it, and if not him, then my friends all worry that they have it.

Between my husband and me, we only have one good head left. One of us is forever forgetting a name, a date, or an event, or else we're losing eyeglasses, car keys, or the book we were just reading. We can't remember whether we saw that movie, or if we did, what it was about.

If a spouse becomes mentally incompetent, the question then is: do I place him or her in a nursing home, or do I keep my spouse at home with, hopefully, some outside help? I have friends who have done both, and either choice can work equally well. Retiring to an independent-living facility that has both assisted living and nursing care available is easier on the caregiver. This way one spouse could be living independently in one accommodation and visit the other on the next floor or in the next building. Proximity to a loved one is important. If a retirement facility is not an option, there are daycare centers that offer relief to the caregiver.

None of us remembers our parents being so forgetful, or if they were, they didn't seem to worry about it. They had less information to store in their memories. There was less global news to worry about, less knowledge about potential environmental disasters. My parents didn't have books on child rearing, they ate meat and potatoes, drank wine with every meal, smoked, and stayed up late, not knowing about vitamins or what foods to eat to prevent heart disease or diabetes. They did not know that cooked tomatoes contain lycopene, an essential nutrient to help prevent prostate cancer. They paid no attention to dark leafy greens, did not know soy existed, and did not count calories. The term probably did not exist in their milieu. There were no endangered species or potential environmental disasters, and since there were no computers, no one ever said to them: "I can't help you now, my computer is down." But I worry about all the above and then some.

Most of us are constantly on "overload." Thanks to television, I know about murders in the South, floods in the Midwest, courtroom cases in the East, and the coming storms from the North. I know the latest on brain research, construction of the dam on the Yangtze River, and starvation in Africa.

Not only was my parents' generation not privy to this information, they wouldn't have cared. We know more than we need to know, and the result is that we keep forgetting stuff and worry that there is something wrong with us.

The more information stored in our minds, the more difficult it is to keep our attention focused. Paying attention is what will help us remember, but much of what we do is on automatic pilot: "did I put something away, or did I just mean to do it and then forget?" Unless I pay attention, I won't know.

When too many things are crowding into our brains, some items are dropped off. Our brains are like file cabinets: when they get too full, that next piece of paper just won't fit in. Yet every time something gets lost or forgotten, I wonder if it's Alzheimer's. Most likely it's Old-Timer's (Normal Age-Related Forgetfulness).

I watched a friend's husband deteriorate in a nursing home. I saw my own aunt unable to recognize me and witnessed my daughter's mother-in-law become incompetent.

It's all around us. All my friends are worried, too. With the slightest misstep, panic sets in. Is this an early sign? When should we worry?

There are other conditions that can mimic Alzheimer's, such as depression, nutritional deficiencies, stroke, Parkinson's and Huntington's disease, drug or alcohol abuse, sleep disorders, and thyroid imbalance, most of which can be treated. Diagnosis is difficult, but it is important to eliminate these as a cause for Alzheimer's-like symptons.

So what are the early signs of Alzheimer's?

1. It's normal to forget a friend or a colleague's name and remember it later. But if you don't remember that the person standing before you is your friend or co-worker, it's a bad sign.

2. It's okay to ask the same question a couple of times, but asking it repeatedly over and over or not remembering you already asked it is a bad sign.

3. You may forget to serve the salad you fixed for dinner, but if you forget you ever made it, it's troublesome.

4. We all misplace things, but if we find the car keys in the freezer or our wallet in the oven, we're in trouble.

5. We have all searched in vain for the right word to say, but if we substitute an inappropriate one that makes no sense, then we should worry.

6. Momentary disorientation is normal, but getting lost on your own street is not.

7. It's okay if you forget to write a check, but if you don't know what a check is used for, then you should be concerned.

8. It's okay to be moody occasionally, but people with Alzheimer's have mood swings for no apparent reason and can become irritable, suspicious, fearful, and confused without cause.

9. It's okay to want to be alone sometimes, but Alzheimer's sufferers can become passive, lack initiative, and refuse to participate in family events or social activities they used to enjoy.

10. And finally, you should feel free to dress as you like, but wearing several shirts, no shoes, or dressing inappropriately could signal Alzheimer's.

One of the more disturbing and painful aspects of this disease is witnessing a loved one slowly deteriorate in front of your eyes and being helpless to prevent it. Also, losing a loved one to dementia adds a different kind of burden: the person you knew is gone, yet their body is there, so you can't officially mourn a death. Yet it is the death of a mind and the end of the companionship of a parent or spouse. It is a departure without the leaving. There is no memorial service, yet the loss is as great, if not greater, than an actual death.

The caregiver is also at risk for depression and exhaustion. Because Alzheimer's patients require twenty-four-hour care, it's important for the caregivers to get some respite. They can experience physical, emotional, social, and financial stresses, and the burden may sometimes seem unbearable for them. Consequently, care for the caregiver is essential. There are several places that can provide information, including ADEAR (Alzheimer's Disease Education and Referral), the local Alzheimer's Association in your area, Eldercare Locator, and the website www.caregiving.com, which provides free, online resources, including support groups, tips and information, and links to other websites about caregiving.

There is hope that in the new millennium we will be able to prevent this terrible disease. Research seems promising. In the meantime, don't worry. You're not losing it. Just keep going and keep stimulating your brain with new adventures. It will be so grateful that it will probably grow a few more synapses for you.

Contact information for organizations mentioned in this chapter:

- ADEAR (Alzheimer's Disease Education and Referral): P.O. Box 8250, Silver Spring, MD 20907-8250, www.alzheimers.org; 800-438-4380

- Alzheimer's Association (they can give you information regarding a local chapter in your area): 225 N. Michigan Ave., Fl.17, Chicago, IL 60601, www.alz.org; 800-272-3900

- Eldercare Locator: www.eldercare.gov; 800-677-1116

- www.caregiving.com

Sometimes I Forget

Sometimes
when I dial a phone number
by the time someone answers
I forget whom it was I was calling

Sometimes
when I write a note to myself
to answer a call or a letter
I forget where I put it

Sometimes when I leave the house
I forget whether I left the lights on
or turned the stove off

Sometimes
I have to check if my toothbrush is wet
to know whether I had already
brushed my teeth that morning

Sometimes on my way home
I drive right by my house
and only notice it a few blocks later

Sometimes
I forget whether I meant to say something
or whether I have already said it

But often
I remember the kind words
the sweet smells
sunlit days
a tender touch
a book I loved
music, a picture
a special event

I guess I remember more than I forget

CHAPTER 12

Living Alone

Transitions

*After one door closes
and before a new one opens
it can be awfully dark
in the hallway*

*But if you stay there
long enough
you'll see a crack of light
under the door*

*Push open and enter
into your new life*

It's not possible to write a book on retirement without mentioning widowhood. Even though my husband and I wish we could die together, it is an unlikely scenario. Managing life alone after a lifetime of togetherness is about as tough as it gets. I know I could not begin to fix things around the house the way my husband does, and every week another thing goes wrong. I am not on top of our finances, though every year I say I plan to learn. Meanwhile, if my husband were left alone, he could not pick up the phone and make a date with friends, get tickets for anything, remember to take his vitamin pills, or prepare a balanced meal. At least he knows how to run the washing machine.

Statistics tell us that people living alone are more prone to illness. This is not surprising, since we are social animals and need intimacy in relationships. Being part of a community helps. Volunteering or joining groups, be they book clubs, athletic clubs, art classes, or political organizations, promotes meeting people with similar interests.

One of the more devastating events of growing older, besides loss of a spouse, is loss of independence, and by this, I mean driving. In a city, not being able to drive is not a problem, due to the available public transportation, but in the suburbs or smaller towns, if you don't drive you can't go anywhere.

We are a car-addicted country, and the fact that older drivers are the most accident-prone age group is lost on people who should not be driving anymore. Certain medications such as pain relievers, sleeping pills, muscle relaxants, and antihistamines all may slow reaction time.[1] What to do? If the driver is not aware of any problems, the person who sits in the passenger seat holding his or her breath with every dangerous move should insist that the driver have a doctor's assessment or a driving test with the state's licensing examiner.

When my father could not drive to the beach anymore, he hired a college student to take him three mornings a week. It's important to get out of the house. If you have stopped driving, find friends who do, especially if there is no public transportation near your house. Make friends with younger people; they will be able to drive for more years.

As a woman grows older, her pool of available men grows smaller. As a man grows older his pool of available women grows larger. It's unfair, but it's the reality.

---

[1] *Mayo Clinic Health Letter* (May 2002).

So if you are a single, retired woman, your problem won't be what to do with yourself during the day, but being lonely in the evening. It is still difficult for a single woman to call up men or even a couple to make a date.

If you are a single, retired man, evenings will not be a problem because all you have to do is pick up the phone and you will have a date. If you don't know anyone to call, your married friends will know single women to introduce you to. It is the daytime that will have to be filled with something other than work.

So how do women deal with evenings and men with daytime? Not easily.

Women need to develop friendships with other single women so they can go together to evening events, and men ought to find meaningful activities to fill their days.

If you have an option as to when to retire, don't do it until you have not only a viable financial plan, but also a plan for your daily activities, your weekly and monthly occupations, and what you will accomplish by the end of the first year.

Married women should learn about their financial situation before they are potentially left alone. Finding oneself widowed and having to cope with money matters after a lifetime of relying on a husband can be a nightmare. In preparing for retirement, one must be ready to do it alone.

The same goes for married men. Being left alone after a lifetime of relying on a wife to run a household and be in charge of your social life can be the same nightmare. I am talking, of course, of my generation in which roles were more gender specific. The younger couples are better at sharing everything equally.

It is easier to retire together, but all too often, one retires alone. Be prepared for that eventuality, too. I need to teach my husband how to make a social engagement, and he needs to teach me how to file a tax return.

Time for Yourself

Sometime
take the time
to sit quietly
and read a book

Sometime
go to an afternoon movie
enroll in a course
or attend a lecture on music or art

Sometime
chat with a friend
about absolutely nothing
or shop when you don't need anything

Sometime
taking the time
to waste time
is not time wasted

CHAPTER 13

Our Middle-Aged Children

Warped Time

If parents don't have enough time for their children
when their children are young
the children won't have enough time for their parents
when their parents are old

What about the kids? Yes, those middle-aged children of ours with families of their own. How do they fit into the picture? They are the "Sandwich Generation," having to take care of their own growing children and also their aging parents (that's us).

Some children find pleasure in helping out an older parent: relationships can become closer and former disagreements become irrelevant. For some children, it can be a burden, especially if the parent lives a distance away and is in ill health. My mother died at ninety-six. I live in San Diego; she lived in Beverly Hills. My husband and I drove to Los Angeles just about every weekend to check on her health, her help situation, her mail, her finances, and the old house, which needed constant repairs. We took her to doctors, to the bank, shopping, and out to eat.

Most of her friends had died and she was very lonely, with only her two around-the-clock nurses to keep her company. She had Parkinson's and fell a lot. My feelings were mixed. Yes, I was glad to be able to help, felt very responsible, and enjoyed being with her, even though I had to shout because her hearing aid was more often in the drawer than in her ear. It was a rare privilege to still have a mother at my age. On the other hand, it was tough battling the Los Angeles traffic, and I missed being home on weekends. Of course I'm happy I did it, but I also felt there was no choice. She was adamant about staying in the house where she had lived for fifty years.

Talking to your children honestly about expectations as you age is extremely important. You need to discuss all possibilities: "What will happen if my spouse dies; what if we become physically disabled or mentally incapacitated; what if we need nursing care; what if...?"

I know that children often refuse to talk about these eventualities, but you must insist. Your wishes must be heard, and they must be willing to engage in your long-range plans. You must prepare for who will do what, under what circumstances, and for whom. In the meantime, you can take care of the grandchildren for a few days, and let the children go on a holiday!

But there is another issue often talked about but rarely written about: the parent who plans to retire and who has a child working in the family business.

Some of these children, who are middle-aged, complain bitterly about being overly supervised and lacking autonomy and trust. One young woman with an MBA writes that her about-to-be-retired mother checks up on her work more than she does on that of any other employee.

We may well ask whether it is the children who cannot accept any authority from the parents with whom they so recently struggled to gain their independence, or whether it is the parents who cannot let go of controlling their children.

Let us examine the dynamics of both possibilities.

One of the major tasks of growing up is growing away from our parents. For young people to be able to stand on their own two feet, they must be able to differentiate themselves from their parents. They need to test parental value systems, lifestyles, beliefs, and goals to see if these fit their own emerging values and styles. They do this by trying out different beliefs and ways of living and by having friends their parents disapprove of. We call this adolescent rebellion.

Even though children may be well beyond the so-called "rebellious years," remnants of this time spent distancing themselves may remain for years. Even though I'm in my seventies and my mother was in her mid-nineties, I was still sometimes startled at the strength of my reactions when she criticized me. This is a mother-daughter dynamic that lasts a lifetime.

It's no wonder a child may resist any attempt from a parent, no matter how legitimate, to control. It could be a helpful suggestion that is taken as criticism or a mild criticism that is perceived as strong disapproval. The push for autonomy from our parents is so strong that any supervision is felt as overly controlling.

Children want to please their parents and care so much about what they think that they exaggerate, in their own minds, any parental reaction that is less than absolutely positive. Every child, from infancy through adulthood, wears a little invisible sign around his or her neck that says: "Mom, Dad, please admire me!"

The other possibility — that, indeed, the parent is a very difficult boss — also needs exploring. Mothers and fathers were always the heads of their families. As children grow older, it is difficult to see them as adults. I still give unsolicited psychological advice to my fifty-three-year-old daughter, who has a PhD in psychology, and business advice to my fifty-one-year-old son with an MBA from Harvard.

Parents remember all the foolish things their kids used to say and do and still attribute them to their grown sons and daughters. They still believe that their own judgment must be better than their children's. If a child takes a position different from a parent, that parent may feel betrayed: family loyalty gets confused with work decisions.

If children do well, it's a chip off the old block. If they don't, then it is perceived as worse than the actual performance warrants. Other employees often believe that bosses' children are unfairly given certain advantages and may resent it, adding to the problem.

Parents do tend to over-supervise their own children. Whereas a mother or father may overlook an employee's minor errors, they notice every mistake their son or daughter makes and may overreact. In other words, the expectations of performance are higher for children, thus placing additional burdens on these children who feel under observation all the time.

Some parents exaggerate their children's achievements and give them responsibilities too soon; some parents underrate their children and continue to keep them in subordinate positions longer than is warranted. Either way, it has little to do with reality.

Parents generally have trouble giving up control. When it's time to retire, many stay on and become burdens to their children, who would normally pension-off aging workers, but cannot because they're "Mom" or "Dad."

A word here about the proverbial overprotective mother, the one who controls, gives contradictory messages, induces guilt, and always complains. This kind of obtrusive and meddling mother is also the very caring, loving mother who would give her life to her children. She is difficult to deal with when she retires, as she wants to stay involved.

With most fathers, it is also a different issue. The older "buck" locks horns with the younger upstart who then wins the fight and inherits the territory. This is true of most animals and true of us. It is indeed difficult for the older man, who may have started his own business or was its head for many years, to give up his creation or his position to his own child who was a baby not that long ago — or so it seems. These problems may exist not only in work situations, but also in family relationships with similar tensions.

Giving up control and letting the child make the decisions, as well as possible mistakes, is very difficult indeed for a lot of men. It does not even have to be your own kid, it can be any younger person who will take over. The dynamics are similar, especially if it is an underling you have mentored. Staying on as a consultant may work in some situations, but all too often the newly-in-charge person will not welcome suggestions from the recently retired older man, who then feels dismissed, overlooked, and unappreciated, and whose "sage" advice goes unheeded.

For both men and women, there is really only one solution to the problems of parents and children in the same business: to talk openly about the retiree's need for control and the younger person's need for autonomy. If it is your child who is taking over, there must be constant reassurance about loyalty, commitment, and love. Although these should not be at stake because of a different opinion at work, they often are and that, of course, is most of the problem. If relationships at work are too fraught with tension, it may be important for the child to prove himself or herself elsewhere before the parent can accept that child as a valuable member of the team and a potential replacement for the parent.

Letting go is difficult enough, but to give up control and see another not follow exactly in your footsteps may feel like a betrayal of a lifelong endeavor. This is why it is so important to move on and accept that in the past, things were done your way, but in the future, they will be done another way — someone else's way.

So let go and move on, because it is only when you can let go of the past that you become ready to explore the future.

Growing

*An infant changes
from minute to minute*

*A baby
from hour to hour*

*A toddler changes
overnight*

*A child
is different each week*

*An adolescent
is new each month*

*A young adult can take
a year to grow*

*I am a senior citizen
and what you see is what you get*

The "Sandwich Generation"

*Being in between
parents who have become like children
and need you
and children who are still just that
and need you*

CHAPTER 14

Important Documents

Why Not?

When something bad
happens to us
we often ask
"Why me?"

Yet we seldom ask
"Why me?"
when something good
happens to us

But on both occasions
what we really ought to ask is
"Why not me?"

You probably will not like this chapter. Have you bought your burial plot? Have you arranged for your funeral? Do you want to leave all this for your children to do after your demise? Suppose it happens suddenly. Will they have to fly in from some distant place and start shopping for a cemetery and a priest, minister, or rabbi? I believe it's an unnecessary burden to place on others. My husband and I have written each other's obituaries, decided on the music, given a list of newspapers to contact to the person in charge at the funeral home, and chosen the caskets and the headstones. All our kids have to do is show up.

After all, we prepare for all kinds of possible catastrophes, such as fires, burglaries, and accidents — none of which may happen, but death will. That's a guarantee, so it is intelligent to prepare for that, too.

It is also a guarantee that if we live long enough, we will grow older. We will not become stronger and more able, so planning for the eventuality of disability, whether physical or mental, is equally important.

Begin by collecting all the important information your family members or caretakers may need. Write down the names and phone numbers of doctors, lawyers, financial advisors, and close friends or relatives who should be contacted in case of an emergency. Make a list of documents, including birth and marriage certificates, insurance policies, Social Security cards, wills, bank and investment account information, property ownership information, income tax returns, and bills. This list should also include the location and content of safe-deposit boxes and irreplaceable family possessions, such as photos or letters. Your children, your accountant, and your lawyer should know where everything is and be updated of any changes. An excellent source for help in financial planning and record keeping is Elderweb at www.elderweb.com.

Additionally, you will need four documents:

1. A living will (also called a healthcare directive), which a lawyer does not need to prepare. It is a directive to your physician specifying whether you want to avoid life-support equipment if you are terminally ill. You must sign your documents or have them signed for you in the presence of witnesses or a notary public — sometimes both, depending on

your state laws. Give copies to your doctor and family members. This should be updated every five years.

2. A durable power of attorney for healthcare. This means you are granting someone else the power to act in your place if you become incapacitated. It is limited to healthcare directives. It is a legally binding document. My husband and I named each other, and if we are unable to perform this responsibility, we have named our children.

3. A durable power of attorney for financial asset management. It's the same as above, except that it is to take care of money matters in case you are no longer able to. Both documents need to be witnessed by two people and notarized. It is recommended that you repeat this process every five years.

4. And finally, your last will and testament. You have many options so you should consult an estate lawyer about your plans, but have something in place to avoid probate and heirs fighting among themselves. Remember to make provisions for the care of your pets if they should outlive you.

Taking care of the above will give you peace of mind. Once it's done, you don't have to think about it, and peace of mind is part of any retirement plan.

Contact information for organizations mentioned in this chapter:

• Elderweb: www.elderweb.com

The Living Will

You have to have one
for directives
to resuscitate or not
to have feeding tubes
and breathing tubes
and other
not-known-to-me tubes
or not

My kids have
a copy but probably lost it
I think my lawyer has one
and my doctor, too
If I remember correctly
at home I filed mine under "L"
for "living" or was it
under "W" for "will"
or perhaps under "M"
for "medical"

Whatever...
You need to have a living will
and more important
you need to remember
where you put it

CHAPTER 15

Trying to Age Gracefully

"That's Me!"

It's the crow's feet
around my eyes
and the puffiness
below them

It's the furrows
on my forehead
and the wrinkles
on my neck

They make me
place my hands
upon my temples
pull back and say
"See, this is how I would
look with a face-lift"

And a face
ten years younger appears
but it's not mine
Then I let go
and smile at the familiar one
knowing that's me
trying to grow older
gracefully

When I look in the mirror, I see an old woman. This always surprises me, because I expect someone much younger to appear. The person I see has a lot of wrinkles, and if I make the mistake of looking into a magnifying mirror, the wrinkles look very deep and the surrounding skin cracked. In other words, my skin is not smooth anymore.

My eyes have receded into my head, and my eyelids droop over them. Also my eyebrows are right above my eyes with no space in between. I don't pluck them because to have a thin line right over my lids would look weird. Some people are prone to dark circles under their eyes or puffiness. I get both when I'm tired. The jowl line is not smooth anymore — from gravity, I guess.

I don't wear makeup — no mascara because my eyes tend to tear, no powder because I have dry skin. So I just put a little cream on my face (when I remember). When I go out in the evening, I use a little rouge and fairly pale lipstick, because dark does not look right with an old face. The neck is my worst part. It's not only wrinkled, but there is a funny piece of skin that hangs there. My father had it, and my mother and my grandmother, too. I have a genetic turkey wattle! Can't wear sleeveless anymore. The skin of my upper arms looks a bit loose, even though I lift weights. Maybe I would be worse off if I didn't exercise.

I had a very small waist when I was young — really small. I used to emphasize it with tight belts and form-fitting dresses. Well, I lost it! I don't know where it went; it just isn't there anymore. So now I wear skirts with an elastic waistband and a top to go over.

I also used to have a flat stomach. Now when I hold it in, it doesn't look so bad but I can't breathe. My bottom is too big and my thighs have spider veins, which makes wearing shorts problematic. I still like my breasts, but if I lose weight (which I should) what will happen to them? My hair is white, but I find that attractive. I used to be a flaming redhead, but I think that the way it is now fits a wrinkled face better. So that's the inventory.

I have several more clues that tell me I'm getting older. I can't walk as fast or as long as I used to. Even though the doctor says my hearing is normal, all of San Diego has begun to mumble, especially around dinner tables when eight or ten people converse at once. I pretend to understand and wonder whether my smiling nods are appropriate when unintelligible comments are addressed to me. Perhaps someone is talking about a war somewhere or an illness, and I happily grin approvingly.

My mother died at ninety-six and my aunt at ninety-eight. They were lonely because most of their friends had died. It's important to have some younger friends, too, so that someone remains when all others are gone.

On the other hand, at seventy-eight, I feel wiser, more competent, and better able to appreciate daily events, like a walk, a nice meal, a chat with a friend, a book, a nap, my husband's arm around me, a joke, or our dog licking the cat's nose. Because I have read that brains can keep growing forever as long as we do something challenging, I have taken up piano lessons (last one was when I was eight years old and my mother said it was hopeless). I can play *Für Elise*. I am also becoming proficient at the computer. I get on the Internet and send e-mails to the grandchildren and even have a scanner to send photographs.

I find this time in my life the most delightful of all. I teach in other people's classes and don't have papers to grade or exams to correct. I give talks on my latest books, *Too Wise to Want to Be Young Again* and *If I Eat I Feel Guilty, If I Don't I'm Deprived*, and get great pleasure from the appreciation I receive. I don't know whether the best is yet to come, but I do know that pretty good has already arrived. At seventy-eight, I'm over the hill with the best view of the years yet to come.

Where does that leave me? Many of my friends are having plastic surgery. One friend had a chemical peel and when I visited her, she had a red and swollen face and a lot of pain. Not for me! Another friend had a face-lift, which made her mouth look stretched with an unnatural smile. I also have several friends who came out of it looking wonderful. But how do you know ahead of time? Going voluntarily under the knife with general anesthesia, antibiotics, and an uncertain outcome is too scary for me, yet my friends who have done it are thrilled with their new looks.

It seems to me that looking young is not in the face but in the movement of the body, the sparkle in the eyes, the energy in the conversation, the passion in the ideas, and the intensity of the emotions. Looking young may not even be the goal. How about looking one's age, mature, wise, fun, fascinating, interested, and interesting, with the wealth of your life's experiences at your fingertips?

At a party, I tend to go toward an interesting-looking older person — wrinkles and all — rather than a smooth-faced, bellybutton-showing young person. I don't notice the age spots, but do notice the breadth or depth of knowledge. I'm more interested in talking about the latest book, rather than the latest face cream.

And so, let us celebrate our advancing years. If we don't want wrinkles and gray hair, we'll have to die young. I am retired from full-time, paid work, but I'm not retired from learning, from commitments, from being available to family and friends, from loving, from life! This is my New Year's resolution: I will not improve this year.

I Noticed that I'm Growing Older

If I get up only once
in the middle of the night
to go to the bathroom
that's a good night
When I wake up in the morning
I have pains in places I didn't know existed
It takes a long time to count all the pills
I take with breakfast every day

The clothes in my closet
keep getting smaller
and so does the print in papers and books
When I have been sitting
for a long time
it takes equally long
to straighten up afterwards
A lot of people in my phone book
have names ending with MD
or are crossed out because they died

I need glasses to find my glasses
and regularly misplace everything else
The children look middle-aged
and worry when I don't call them
I joined a health club and never went
put on a tape to do aerobics
and just sat and watched it
On airplanes, I'm asked if I want to board early
In crowded places, I'm given a seat
and automatically get the senior discounts

I forget what I'm talking about
in the middle of my own sentence
I can't recall the name of the person
introduced to me thirty seconds ago
I look forward to a quiet evening at home
when I can fall asleep watching
the ten o'clock news
I just noticed that I'm growing older

Conclusion

"Be Thyself"

Socrates said
"Know thyself"
let us add
"Be thyself"
which is much more
difficult to do
because we often are
what others want us
to be

Whether you're deciding about retirement, planning on it, or are retired, this can be the best time of your life. There is a reason it's called the golden years: you finally have a chance to be totally yourself, free of many of the obligations that work and growing families required. You can indulge in a variety of pursuits for the fun of it or not.

Hopefully, you don't have financial worries, grown kids to still support, illness in the family, and world news to upset you. Hopefully, you are free not only to continue your life, but to expand it in all kinds of new directions.

What we have needed in our younger years, we still need as we grow older:

Physical activity

Mental challenges

Good healthcare

Freedom of choice

A sense of security

Good friends, both for comfort and for fun

And most of all:

A willingness to try new things

As we lose our youth, we gain maturity. As we lose friends, we learn to make new ones. As members of our family die, we remain with the memories of the good times together. We may lose health, an active lifestyle, and much of what we have loved, but loss is the inevitable toll we pay for living.

All along our great adventure, we have grown in understanding and life experiences. Along the way, we had to reinvent ourselves to cope, but at every turn of the road, we were met with the next challenge. Now comes our greatest challenge of all: taking the time to become who we really are.

Retirement is that opportunity. Let your great adventure begin. And let us all celebrate life as a gift, not as a given.

When
One Door Closes

Old doors are closing behind me
those of youth
invulnerability
independence
immortality

But new doors are opening in front of me
those of wisdom
focused energies
trusting friendships
moments savored

The Next Great Adventure

As we lose our youth
we gain maturity
We learn to let go
of the past
in order to step into the future
At every turn of the road
we were met with new challenges
and now comes
the greatest challenge of all:
finding ourselves
in order to become
who we really are
Retirement is
that opportunity
Retirement is
our next great adventure!

The Obsolete Rules I Live By

*F*inish everything on my plate
and always use all leftovers

Do not spend money on myself
unless absolutely necessary

Don't throw out old clothes that still fit
or may fit again someday when I lose weight

Keep everything potentially useful
even if I haven't used it for the past 20 years

Write thank-you notes
the same day I receive a present

Make up my bed every morning
even if no one is expected to come into the bedroom

And finally, keep all magazines, newsletters,
articles, and the latest medical updates
in a large pile under my desk to read later when I have time

ABOUT THE AUTHOR

Photo by Herman Gadon

Natasha Josefowitz calls herself a late bloomer, having earned her master's degree at age forty and her PhD at age fifty. She is an adjunct professor at the School of Social Work at San Diego State University, a noted columnist, and the author of seventeen books, including *Too Wise to Want to Be Young Again: A Witty View of How to Stop Counting the Years and Start Living Them* and *If I Eat I Feel Guilty, If I Don't I'm Deprived ...and Other Dilemmas of Daily Life*, both published by Blue Mountain Arts, Inc.

Dr. Josefowitz is an internationally-known speaker, having lived and worked abroad and in the U.S. For ten years, she had her own weekly radio broadcast and a weekly television segment. Her efforts on behalf of women have earned her numerous awards, including *The Living Legacy Award* from the Women's International Center and *The Women Helping Women Award* from the Soroptimist International. She has been named *Woman of the Year* five times by various national and international organizations, including the Women's Management Association, and was also honored by California Women in Government for her contributions to education.

Natasha is the mother and stepmother of five children; she has seven grandchildren, three step-grandchildren, and five step-great-grandchildren. She is white-haired, wrinkled, and has a few extra pounds, but says she can celebrate life because she has PMZ (Post-Menopausal Zest).